INTRODUCTION

Since the pages of this book was digitalized from a very old original,
the pages here may look a little funny at times.
Rest assured we did our best to format the original book
into modern form as best allowed by the current processes available.

Although each page of this book was copied from the original edition,
this reprint is in no way endorsed by or associated with the original author Leo Engel.

Ross Brown

Introduction and Cover Art Copyright 2008 -
All rights reserved.
TheDesignHouse
ISBN 1440451893

For regular updates on new reprint editions of
vinatge cocktail books,
vintage wine books,
vintage drinks books and
vintage cooking books
please visit

www.VintageCocktailBooks.com

PREFACE.

————:o:————

"OH! that men should put an enemy in their mouths to steal
away their brains !" These few words, culled from a work of the
immortal Shakespeare, must speak volumes in favour of those
"Cooling Drinks" so artistically concocted to tickle the palate of
mankind. The Americans, to whom we are indebted for a great
number of ingenious inventions that have added greatly to the
comfort of the human race, were the first to introduce these wholesome and invigorating Refreshers. For many years they only
flourished in the United States, but have at last become acclima-
tized in every quarter of the globe, and are now the acknowledged
drink at all Bacchanalian revels. Every great city now boasts of
its "Alabama Fog-cutters," its "Connecticut Eye-openers," its
"Thunderbolt Cocktails," its "Lightning Smashers," its "Boston
Nose-warmers," its "Magnetic Crushers," its "Galvanic Lip-
pouters," its "Josey Ticklers," and its "Leo Coaxers." It occurred
to the author of this work that it was only right that the public
should be made acquainted with the precise manner in which these
drinks are manipulated, there being a vast difference in both their
flavour and effect if made from a proper recipe. Leo, during
his lengthened sojourn in America, collected an unlimited number
of original and other recipes for "Drinks," and has become a great

benefactor to the British nation. Parr or Morison may have contributed by their skill to health, but it has been reserved for Leo to look after both health and spirits ; and we feel certain that no one will deny that the social drinks he has popularized in this country have added to the comfort and enjoyment of all classes of the community, from His Royal Highness the Prince of Wales to the most humble of Her Gracious Majesty's subjects. It is our intention to select from his gigantic catalogue of recipes upwards of two hundred various compounds, each of which has been extensively patronized by the bon vivants of every country, and to explain in this little volume the best method of concocting them ; so that in the future there will be no excuse for any one that happens to have this book in the library ever again imbibing any of those "villainous compounds" so often to be met with. Having made this liberal promise, we shall now take our leave, make our bow, and, like the Peri in Lalla Rookh, exclaim—

> Joy, joy for ever, my task is done ;
> The gate is passed, the haven is won.

CONTENTS.

—:o:—

The Table of Contents refers to the number of each Recipe not to the folios of the pages.

—:o:—

CONTENTS.

1

American and Other Drinks.

—————⟩◆⟨—————

PUNCH.

——:o:——

THERE is a fine old English poet who enlightens us by saying that

"Punch cures the Gout, the Cholic, and the Phthisic,
And it is to all men the very best of Physic."

If it really possess the wonderful powers ascribed to it, of which
we have no reason to doubt, it becomes us, in the first place, to say
how to make this delicious beverage in perfection. When you
have carefully selected some lemons or limes, their ambrosial
essence must be extracted by rubbing lumps of sugar on the
rind, which break the delicate little vessels that contain the per-
fume and, at the same time, absorb it. The great secret in
Punch brewing is to make the mixture sweet and strong, using tea
instead of water, and so thoroughly amalgamating all the compounds that the taste of neither the bitter, the sweet, the spirit,
nor the element shall be perceptible one over the other. Should
you wish to make hot Punch, you put in the spirits before the
water; and if cold Punch, then the water or tea first.

1   BRANDY PUNCH.

Use large tumbler.

One table-spoonful of raspberry syrup; two tea-spoonfuls of white
powdered sugar; one wine glass of water; one and a half wine
glass of brandy; one and a half small lemons; two slices of
orange; one piece of pine-apple. Fill the tumbler with chipped
ice, shake well, and dress the top with berries in season. Sip
through a straw.

2   BRANDY PUNCH.

For a Party of Ten.

Half gallon of water; one and a half quart of brandy; quarter
pint of Jamaica rum; juice of three large lemons; two oranges
sliced; half a pine-apple pared and cut up; half gill of orange
Curaçoa; one gill of raspberry syrup. Ice, and add berries in
season. Mix the materials well together in a large bowl, and dress
with fruits in season according to taste.

3   MISSOURI PUNCH.

Use large tumbler.

One wine glass of brandy; half a wine glass of Jamaica rum; the
same of Bourbon whiskey; the same of water; one and a half table-
spoonful of powdered white sugar; table-spoonful of lemon juice,
fill up with chipped ice. The above must be well shaken; and
those who like their draughts "like linked sweetness long drawn
out," should use a straw to sip the nectar through. The top of
this punch should be ornamented with small pieces of fruit and
berries in season.

4   IRISH WHISKEY PUNCH.

This is the genuine Irish beverage. It is generally made one-
third pure whiskey, two-thirds boiling water, in which the sugar
has been dissolved, and lemon peel according to taste.

5 SCOTCH WHISKEY—APPOLONIC PUNCH.

Steep some thin yellow shavings of lemon peel in the whiskey, which should be pure Islày of the best quality. The sugar should be dissolved in boiling water. Proportions as in Irish Whiskey Punch (No. 4).

6 GIN PUNCH.
Use large tumbler.

One table-spoonful of raspberry syrup; the same of white sugar; one wine glass of water; one and a half wine glass of gin; half small-sized lemon; two slices of orange. Fill the tumbler with shaved ice, shake well, and ornament the top with berries in season. Sip through a straw.

7 GIN PUNCH.
Another.

Half pint of old gin; one gill of Maraschino; the juice of three lemons; the rind of half a lemon; one quart bottle of German seltzer water. Ice well and sweeten to taste.

8 CHAMPAGNE PUNCH.

A quart bottle of Champagne; two ounces of sugar; one orange sliced; the juice of a lemon; three slices of pine-apple; one wine glass of raspberry or strawberry syrup. Ornament with fruits in season, and serve in Champagne goblets. This can be made in any quantity by observing the proportions of the ingredients as given above. Four bottles of Champagne make a gallon, and this is generally sufficient for fifteen persons in a mixed party.

9 CLARET PUNCH.
Use large tumbler.

One and a half tea-spoonful of sugar; one slice of lemon; two or three slices of orange. Fill the tumbler with chipped ice, and then pour in the claret. Shake well and ornament with fruit in season. Place a straw in the glass.

10   SAUTERNE PUNCH.

Use large tumbler.

The same as No. 9, but with Sauterne instead of claret.

11   PORT WINE PUNCH.

Use large tumbler.

The same as No, 9, using port wine instead of claret, and ornament with berries in season.

12   VANILLA PUNCH.

Use large tumbler.

One table-spoonful of sugar; one wine glass of brandy; one table-spoonful of lemon juice. Fill the tumbler with shaved ice, shake well, ornament with one or two slices of lemon, and flavour with a few drops of Vanilla extract. This is a delicious drink, and should be imbibed through a glass tube or straw, the former being the better.

13   PINE-APPLE PUNCH.

For a Party of Ten.

Four bottles of Champagne; one pint of Jamaica rum; one pint of brandy; one gill of orange Curaçoa; the juice of four lemons; four pine-apples sliced; sweeten with a gill of plain syrup. Put the pine-apple, with one pound of sugar, in a bowl, and let them stand until the sugar is well soaked into the pine-apple, then add all the ingredients, except the Champagne; place a large block of ice in the centre of the bowl, then add the Champagne, pouring it into the bowl at the side, so that it may effervesce as little as possible, and ornament with loaf sugar, sliced orange, and fruits in season; serve in Champagne glasses as soon as made. Pine-apple Punch is sometimes made by adding sliced pine-apple to Brandy Punch.

14 ORGEAT PUNCH.

Use large tumbler.

One and a half table-spoonful of Orgeat syrup ; one and a half wine glass of brandy ; the juice of half a lemon. Fill the tumbler with shaved ice, shake well, ornament with berries in season, and dash a little port wine on top.

15 CURAÇOA PUNCH.

Use large tumbler.

One tea-spoonful of sugar ; one wine glass of brandy ; half a wine glass of Jamaica rum ; one wine glass of water ; half liqueur glass of Curaçoa, and the juice of half a lemon. Fill the tumbler with chipped ice, shake well, and ornament with fruits in season. Sip through a straw and *sigh!*

16 MILK PUNCH.

Use large tumbler.

One table-spoonful of fine white sugar ; one table-spoonful of water ; one wine glass of Cognac brandy ; half a wine glass of Santa Cruz rum or Jamaica ; a little chipped ice. Fill with milk, shake the ingredients well together, and grate a little nutmeg on top.

17 HOT MILK PUNCH.

Use large tumbler.

This punch is made the same as No. 16, with the exception that hot milk is used and no ice.

18   CRITERION MILK PUNCH.

Put the following ingredients into a very clean pitcher:—The juice of three lemons, the rind of two lemons; one pound of powdered sugar; one pine-apple, peeled, sliced, and pounded; six cloves; twenty coriander seeds; one small stick of cinnamon; one pint of brandy; one pint of rum; one gill of arrack; one cup of strong green tea; one quart of boiling water; the boiling water to be added last. Cork this down to prevent evaporation, and allow these ingredients to steep for at least six hours, then add a quart of hot milk and the juice of two lemons. Mix and filter through a jelly bag, and when the punch has passed bright, bottle it and cork tightly. This punch should be iced for drinking.

19   ENGLISH MILK PUNCH.

This seductive drink is made in the following manner :—To two quarts of water add one quart of milk ; mix one quart of Jamaica rum with two quarts of French brandy, and put the spirit to the milk, stirring it for a short time ; let it stand for an hour, but do not suffer anyone of delicate appetite to see the mélange in its present state, as the sight might create a distaste for the punch when perfected. Filter through blotting-paper into bottles, and should you find that the liquid be cloudy, which it should not be, you may clarify it by adding a small portion of isinglass to each bottle. The above receipt will furnish you with half a dozen bottles of punch.

20   NEWPORT PUNCH.

Melt half a pound of lump sugar in half a pint of cold water, with the juice of two lemons passed through a fine hair strainer ; this is sherbet, and must be well mingled ; then add old Jamaica rum, one part of rum to five of sherbet ; cut a couple of limes in two, and run each section rapidly round the edge of the jug or bowl, gently squeezing in some of the delicate acid. This done, the punch is made. Imbibe.

21 REGENTS PARK CUP.

For a Party of Twenty.

The ingredients for this renowned cup are—Two bottles of Champagne ; one bottle of Hockheimer ; one bottle of orange Curaçoa ; one bottle of Cognac ; half bottle of Jamaica rum ; two bottles of Madeira ; two bottles of seltzer or plain soda ; four pounds of raisins ; to which add oranges, lemons, rock candy, and instead of water green tea to taste. Refrigerate with all the icy power of the North Pole.

22 RASPBERRY PUNCH.

One and a half gill of raspberry syrup ; three quarters of a pound of lump sugar ; three and a half pints of boiling water. Infuse half an hour, strain, add half a pint of porter, and from three-quarters of a pint to one pint each of rum and brandy ; add more warm water and sugar, if desired to make weaker and sweeter. A liqueur glass of Noyeau or Maraschino improves it.

23 ST. CHARLES PUNCH.

Use large tumbler.

One table-spoonful of sugar ; one wine glass of port wine ; one liqueur glass of brandy ; the juice of the quarter of a lemon ; fill the tumbler with shaved ice, shake well, and ornament with fruits, and serve with a straw.

24 69th REGIMENT PUNCH.

In earthern jug.

Half a wine glass of Irish whiskey ; half a wine glass of Scotch whiskey ; one teaspoonful of sugar ; a piece of lemon ; two wine glasses of hot water. This is a capital punch for a cold night.

25 SARATOGA PUNCH.

For a Party of Twenty.

Three bottles of Champagne, iced ; one bottle of Cognac ; six oranges ; one pine-apple. Slice the oranges and pine-apple in a bowl, pour the Cognac over them, and let them steep for two hours, then add the Champagne, and serve immediately.

26 THE JOSIE PUNCH.

One bottle of Islay whiskey; one bottle of Monongahela whiskey; lemon peel, sugar, and boiling water at discretion.

27 IMPERIAL CUP.

One bottle of claret ; one bottle of soda water; four table-spoonfuls of powdered white sugar ; quarter of a teaspoonful of grated nutmeg ; one liqueur glass of Maraschino ; about half a pound of ice ; three or four slices of cucumber peel. Put all the ingredients into a bowl or pitcher and mix well.

28 VICTORIA PUNCH.

For a Party of Twenty.

Six lemons, in slices ; half a gallon of brandy ; half a gallon of Jamaica rum ; one pound of white sugar ; one and three-quarter quarts of water ; one pint of milk. Steep the lemons for twenty-four hours in the brandy and rum, add the sugar, water, and milk, and then, when well mixed, strain through a jelly bag. This punch may be used either hot or cold. Make in proportion for smaller number.

29 ROCKY MOUNTAIN PUNCH.

For a mixed Party of Twen'.

This delicious punch is compounded as follows :—Five bottles of Champagne ; one quart of Jamaica rum ; one pint of Maraschino ; six lemons, sliced ; sugar to taste. Mix the above ingredients in a

FRUITS USED IN MAKING PUNCH.

large punch-bowl, then place in the centre of the bowl a large square block of ice, ornamented on top with rock candy, loaf sugar, sliced lemons or oranges, and fruits in season. This is a splendid punch for New Year's day.

30 PUNCH GRASSOT.

One wine glass of brandy ; five drops of orange Curaçoa ; one drop of acetic acid ; two tea-spoonfuls of simple syrup ; one tea-spoonful of syrup of strawberries ; quarter of a pint of water ; the peel of a small lemon sliced ; mix. Serve up with ice in large goblet, and if possible garnish the top with a slice of apricot or peach. In cold weather this punch is admirable, served hot.

31 LIGHT GUARD PUNCH.

For a Party of Twenty.

Three bottles of Champagne ; one bottle of pale sherry ; one bottle of Cognac ; one bottle of Sauterne ; one pine-apple, sliced ; four lemons, sliced. Sweeten to taste, mix in a punch-bowl, cool with a large lump of ice, and serve immediately.

32 PHILADELPHIA FISH HOUSE PUNCH.

Half pint of lemon juice ; three-quarters of a pound of white sugar ; one pint of mixture ;* two and a half pints of cold water. *The above is generally enough for one person! ! ! !*

33 CANADIAN PUNCH.

Two quarts of rye whiskey ; one pint of Jamaica rum ; six lemons, sliced ; one pine-apple, sliced ; four quarts of water. Sweeten to taste, and ice.

---

* To make this mixture, take a quarter of a pint of peach brandy, half a pint of Cognac, and a quarter of a pint of Jamaica rum.

34   TIP-TOP CUP.

For a Party of Five.

One bottle of Champagne; two bottles of soda water; one lique‹ glass of orange Curaçoa ; two table-spoonfuls of powdered suga‹ two slices of pine-apple, cut up.   Put all the ingredients in small punch-bowl, mix well, and serve in Champagne goblets.

35   ARRACK PUNCH.

Three wine glasses of Arrack ; two wine glasses of rum. great deal of sugar is required, but must be left to taste ; tv lemons are generally enough for the above quantity, but more ‹ fewer may be used according to palate ; add water to make up tl whole to one pint and a half, and you then have three tumble of pretty punch.

36   ARRACK PUNCH.

Another.

Steep, for six hours, in one quart of Batavia Arrack, six lemor cut in thin slices, at the end of which time the lemon must l removed without squeezing ; dissolve one pound of loaf sugar one quart of boiling water, and add the hot solution to the Arracl let it stand to cool. This is a delightful *liqueur*, and should be us‹ as such.

37   BIMBO PUNCH.

Bimbo is made in the same way as No. 36, except that Cogn is substituted for Arrack

38   COLD PUNCH.

Arrack, port wine, and water, of each two pints ; one pound loaf sugar ; and the juice of eight lemons.

39   UNITED SERVICE PUNCH.

Dissolve in two pints of hot tea one pound of sugar, add thereto the juice of six lemons, a pint of Arrack, and a pint of port wine.

40   RUBY PUNCH.

Dissolve in two pints of hot tea three quarters of a pound of loaf sugar, having previously rubbed off with a portion of the sugar the peel of four lemons, then add the juice of eight lemons and a pint of Arrack.

41   ROYAL PUNCH.

One pint of hot green tea ; half a pint of brandy ; half a pint of Jamaica rum ; one wine glass of white Curaçoa ; one wine glass of Arrack ; the juice of two limes ; a thin slice of lemon ; white sugar to taste ; a gill of warm calf's-foot jelly. To be drunk as hot as possible. This is a composition worthy of a king. The materials being admirably blended ; the inebriating effects of the spirits are deadened by the tea, whilst the jelly softens the mixture, and destroys the acrimony of the acid. The whites of two eggs well beaten to a froth may be substituted for the jelly when that is not at hand. If the punch be too strong, add more green tea to taste.

42   CENTURY CLUB PUNCH.

Two parts old Santa Cruz rum ; one part old Jamaica rum ; five parts water; lemon and sugar *ad lib*. This is a nice punch.

43   GOTHIC PUNCH.

For a Party of Ten.

Four bottles of Kelly Island Catawba ; one bottle of claret ; three oranges or one pine-apple ; ten table-spoonfuls of sugar. Let this mixture stand in a very cold place, or in ice, for one hour or more, then add one bottle of Champagne.

44 · NORFOLK PUNCH.

In twenty quarts of French brandy put the peels of thirty lemons and thirty oranges, pared so thin that not the least of the white is left, infuse for twelve hours ; have ready thirty quarts of water that have been boiled but allowed to cool, put to it fifteen pounds of re- fined sugar, and when well mixed, pour it upon the brandy and peels, adding the juice of the oranges and of twenty-four lemons ; mix well, then strain through a very fine hair-sieve into a very clean barrel that has held spirits, and put into it two quarts of new milk, stir, and then bung it close. Let it stand six weeks in a warm cellar. Bottle the liquor for use, observing great care that the bottles are perfectly clean and dry, and the corks of the best quality, and well put in. This liquor will keep many years, and improve with age.

45 QUEENS PUNCH

Put two ounces of cream of tartar and the juice and parings of two lemons into a stone jar, pour on them seven quarts of boiling water, stir, and cover close. When cold, sweeten with loaf sugar, and straining it, bottle and cork tight. Add, when bottling, half a pint of rum to the whole quantity. This is a very pleasant and wholesome liquor.

46 UNCLE TOBY PUNCH (English).

Take two large fresh lemons with rough skins, quite ripe, and some large lumps of refined sugar ; rub the sugar over the lemons till it has absorbed all the yellow parts of the skins ; then put into the bowl these lumps, and as much more as the juice of the lemons may be supposed to require, for no certain weight can be mentioned, as the ascidity of the lemon cannot be known till tried, and, therefore, this must be determined by the taste. Then squeeze the lemon juice upon the sugar, and with a bruiser press the sugar and the juice particularly well together, for a great deal of the richness and fine flavour of the punch depend on this

rubbing and mixing process being thoroughly performed. Then mix this up well with boiling water (soft water is best) till the whole is rather cool. When this mixture (which is now called the Sherbet) is to your taste, take brandy and rum in equal quantities and put them to it, again mixing the whole well together. The quantity of spirit must be according to taste. Two good lemons are generally enough to make four quarts of punch, with half a pound of sugar, but this depends much upon the taste and upon the strength of the spirit. As the pulp is disagreeable to some persons, the Sherbet may be strained before the liquor is put in. Some strain the lemon before they put it to the sugar, but that is improper; for when the pulp and sugar are mixed well together, they add much to the richness of the punch. When only rum is used, about half a pint of porter will soften the punch; and even when both rum and brandy are used, the porter gives a richness and, to some, a very pleasant flavour.

47   OXFORD PUNCH.

I have been favoured by an English gentleman with the following recipe for the concoction of punch as drunk by the students of the University of Oxford :—Rub the rinds of three fresh lemons with loaf sugar till you have extracted a portion of the juice ; cut the peel finely off two sweet oranges ; add six glasses of calf's-foot jelly. Let all be put into a large jug and stirred well together. Pour in two quarts of boiling water, and set the jug upon the hob for twenty minutes, strain the liquor through a fine sieve into a large bowl, pour in a bottle of Capillaire,* half a pint of sherry, a pint of Cognac, a pint of old Jamaica rum, a quart of orange shrub, stir well as you pour in the spirit. If you find it requires more sweetness, add sugar to taste.

---

* Receipt for making Capillaire :—To one gallon of water add twenty-eight pounds of loaf sugar, put over the fire to simmer, when milk warm add the whites of four or five eggs, well beaten ; as these simmer with the syrup, skim it well, then pour it off, and flavour with orange-flower water, or bitter almonds, whichever you prefer.

44 . NORFOLK PUNCH.

In twenty quarts of French brandy put the peels of thirty lemons and thirty oranges, pared so thin that not the least of the white is left, infuse for twelve hours ; have ready thirty quarts of water that have been boiled but allowed to cool, put to it fifteen pounds of refined sugar, and when well mixed, pour it upon the brandy and peels, adding the juice of the oranges and of twenty-four lemons ; mix well, then strain through a very fine hair-sieve into a very clean barrel that has held spirits, and put into it two quarts of new milk, stir, and then bung it close. Let it stand six weeks in a warm cellar. Bottle the liquor for use, observing great care that the bottles are perfectly clean and dry, and the corks of the best quality, and well put in. This liquor will keep many years, and improve with age.

45 QUEENS PUNCH

Put two ounces of cream of tartar and the juice and parings of two lemons into a stone jar, pour on them seven quarts of boiling water, stir, and cover close. When cold, sweeten with loaf sugar, and straining it, bottle and cork tight. Add, when bottling, half a pint of rum to the whole quantity. This is a very pleasant and wholesome liquor.

46 UNCLE TOBY PUNCH (English).

Take two large fresh lemons with rough skins, quite ripe, and some large lumps of refined sugar ; rub the sugar over the lemons till it has absorbed all the yellow parts of the skins ; then put into the bowl these lumps, and as much more as the juice of the lemons may be supposed to require, for no certain weight can be mentioned, as the acidity of the lemon cannot be known till tried, and, therefore, this must be determined by the taste. Then squeeze the lemon juice upon the sugar, and with a bruiser press the sugar and the juice particularly well together, for a great deal of the richness and fine flavour of the punch depend on this

rubbing and mixing process being thoroughly performed. Then mix this up well with boiling water (soft water is best) till the whole is rather cool. When this mixture (which is now called the Sherbet) is to your taste, take brandy and rum in equal quantities and put them to it, again mixing the whole well together. The quantity of spirit must be according to taste. Two good lemons are generally enough to make four quarts of punch, with half a pound of sugar, but this depends much upon the taste and upon the strength of the spirit. As the pulp is disagreeable to some persons, the Sherbet may be strained before the liquor is put in. Some strain the lemon before they put it to the sugar, but that is improper; for when the pulp and sugar are mixed well together, they add much to the richness of the punch. When only rum is used, about half a pint of porter will soften the punch; and even when both rum and brandy are used, the porter gives a richness and, to some, a very pleasant flavour.

47 OXFORD PUNCH.

I have been favoured by an English gentleman with the following recipe for the concoction of punch as drunk by the students of the University of Oxford :—Rub the rinds of three fresh lemons with loaf sugar till you have extracted a portion of the juice ; cut the peel finely off two sweet oranges ; add six glasses of calf's-foot jelly. Let all be put into a large jug and stirred well together. Pour in two quarts of boiling water, and set the jug upon the hob for twenty minutes, strain the liquor through a fine sieve into a large bowl, pour in a bottle of Capillaire,* half a pint of sherry, a pint of Cognac, a pint of old Jamaica rum, a quart of orange shrub, stir well as you pour in the spirit. If you find it requires more sweetness, add sugar to taste.

---

* Receipt for making Capillaire :—To one gallon of water add twenty-eight pounds of loaf sugar, put over the fire to simmer, when milk warm add the whites of four or five eggs, well beaten ; as these simmer with the syrup, skim it well, then pour it off, and flavour with orange-flower water, or bitter almonds, whichever you prefer.

44 · NORFOLK PUNCH.

In twenty quarts of French brandy put the peels of thirty lemons
and thirty oranges, pared so thin that not the least of the white is
left, infuse for twelve hours ; have ready thirty quarts of water that
have been boiled but allowed to cool, put to it fifteen pounds of refined sugar, and when well mixed, pour it upon the brandy and peels,
adding the juice of the oranges and of twenty-four lemons ; mix well,
then strain through a very fine hair-sieve into a very clean barrel that
has held spirits, and put into it two quarts of new milk, stir, and
then bung it close. Let it stand six weeks in a warm cellar. Bottle
the liquor for use, observing great care that the bottles are perfectly
clean and dry, and the corks of the best quality, and well put in.
This liquor will keep many years, and improve with age.

45 · QUEENS PUNCH

Put two ounces of cream of tartar and the juice and parings of
two lemons into a stone jar, pour on them seven quarts of boiling
water, stir, and cover close. When cold, sweeten with loaf sugar,
and straining it, bottle and cork tight. Add, when bottling, half a
pint of rum to the whole quantity. This is a very pleasant and
wholesome liquor.

46 · UNCLE TOBY PUNCH (English).

Take two large fresh lemons with rough skins, quite ripe, and
some large lumps of refined sugar ; rub the sugar over the
lemons till it has absorbed all the yellow parts of the skins ; then
put into the bowl these lumps, and as much more as the juice of
the lemons may be supposed to require, for no certain weight can
be mentioned, as the ascidity of the lemon cannot be known till
tried, and, therefore, this must be determined by the taste. Then
squeeze the lemon juice upon the sugar, and with a bruiser press
the sugar and the juice particularly well together, for a great deal
of the richness and fine flavour of the punch depend on this

rubbing and mixing process being thoroughly performed. Then mix this up well with boiling water (soft water is best) till the whole is rather cool. When this mixture (which is now called the Sherbet) is to your taste, take brandy and rum in equal quantities and put them to it, again mixing the whole well together. The quantity of spirit must be according to taste. Two good lemons are generally enough to make four quarts of punch, with half a pound of sugar, but this depends much upon the taste and upon the strength of the spirit. As the pulp is disagreeable to some persons, the Sherbet may be strained before the liquor is put in. Some strain the lemon before they put it to the sugar, but that is improper; for when the pulp and sugar are mixed well together, they add much to the richness of the punch. When only rum is used, about half a pint of porter will soften the punch; and even when both rum and brandy are used, the porter gives a richness and, to some, a very pleasant flavour.

47   OXFORD PUNCH.

I have been favoured by an English gentleman with the following recipe for the concoction of punch as drunk by the students of the University of Oxford :—Rub the rinds of three fresh lemons with loaf sugar till you have extracted a portion of the juice ; cut the peel finely off two sweet oranges ; add six glasses of calf's-foot jelly. Let all be put into a large jug and stirred well together. Pour in two quarts of boiling water, and set the jug upon the hob for twenty minutes, strain the liquor through a fine sieve into a large bowl, pour in a bottle of Capillaire,* half a pint of sherry, a pint of Cognac, a pint of old Jamaica rum, a quart of orange shrub, stir well as you pour in the spirit. If you find it requires more sweetness, add sugar to taste.

---

* Receipt for making Capillaire :—To one gallon of water add twenty-eight pounds of loaf sugar, put over the fire to simmer, when milk warm add the whites of four or five eggs, well beaten ; as these simmer with the syrup, skim it well, then pour it off, and flavour with orange-flower water, or bitter almonds, whichever you prefer.

44 · NORFOLK PUNCH.

In twenty quarts of French brandy put the peels of thirty lemons and thirty oranges, pared so thin that not the least of the white is left, infuse for twelve hours ; have ready thirty quarts of water that have been boiled but allowed to cool, put to it fifteen pounds of refined sugar, and when well mixed, pour it upon the brandy and peels, adding the juice of the oranges and of twenty-four lemons ; mix well, then strain through a very fine hair-sieve into a very clean barrel that has held spirits, and put into it two quarts of new milk, stir, and then bung it close. Let it stand six weeks in a warm cellar. Bottle the liquor for use, observing great care that the bottles are perfectly clean and dry, and the corks of the best quality, and well put in. This liquor will keep many years, and improve with age.

45 · QUEENS PUNCH

Put two ounces of cream of tartar and the juice and parings of two lemons into a stone jar, pour on them seven quarts of boiling water, stir, and cover close. When cold, sweeten with loaf sugar, and straining it, bottle and cork tight. Add, when bottling, half a pint of rum to the whole quantity. This is a very pleasant and wholesome liquor.

46 · UNCLE TOBY PUNCH (English).

Take two large fresh lemons with rough skins, quite ripe, and some large lumps of refined sugar ; rub the sugar over the lemons till it has absorbed all the yellow parts of the skins ; then put into the bowl these lumps, and as much more as the juice of the lemons may be supposed to require, for no certain weight can be mentioned, as the ascidity of the lemon cannot be known till tried, and, therefore, this must be determined by the taste. Then squeeze the lemon juice upon the sugar, and with a bruiser press the sugar and the juice particularly well together, for a great deal of the richness and fine flavour of the punch depend on this

rubbing and mixing process being thoroughly performed. Then mix this up well with boiling water (soft water is best) till the whole is rather cool. When this mixture (which is now called the Sherbet) is to your taste, take brandy and rum in equal quantities and put them to it, again mixing the whole well together. The quantity of spirit must be according to taste. Two good lemons are generally enough to make four quarts of punch, with half a pound of sugar, but this depends much upon the taste and upon the strength of the spirit. As the pulp is disagreeable to some persons, the Sherbet may be strained before the liquor is put in. Some strain the lemon before they put it to the sugar, but that is improper; for when the pulp and sugar are mixed well together, they add much to the richness of the punch. When only rum is used, about half a pint of porter will soften the punch; and even when both rum and brandy are used, the porter gives a richness and, to some, a very pleasant flavour.

47   OXFORD PUNCH.

I have been favoured by an English gentleman with the following recipe for the concoction of punch as drunk by the students of the University of Oxford :—Rub the rinds of three fresh lemons with loaf sugar till you have extracted a portion of the juice ; cut the peel finely off two sweet oranges ; add six glasses of calf's-foot jelly. Let all be put into a large jug and stirred well together. Pour in two quarts of boiling water, and set the jug upon the hob for twenty minutes, strain the liquor through a fine sieve into a large bowl, pour in a bottle of Capillaire,* half a pint of sherry, a pint of Cognac, a pint of old Jamaica rum, a quart of orange shrub, stir well as you pour in the spirit. If you find it requires more sweetness, add sugar to taste.

* Receipt for making Capillaire :—To one gallon of water add twenty-eight pounds of loaf sugar, put over the fire to simmer, when milk warm add the whites of four or five eggs, well beaten ; as these simmer with the syrup, skim it well, then pour it off, and flavour with orange-flower water, or bitter almonds, whichever you prefer.

48   PUNCH A LA ROMAINE.

For a Party of Fifteen.

Take the juice of ten lemons and two sweet oranges; dissolve
in it two pounds of powdered sugar, and add the thin rind of
an orange; run this through a sieve, and stir in by degrees the
whites of ten eggs beaten into a froth. Put the bowl with the mixture into an ice pail, let it freeze a little, then stir briskly into it a
bottle of Champagne and a bottle of Rum.

49   TEA PUNCH.

Make an infusion of the best green tea, an ounce to a quart of
boiling water. Put before the fire a silver or other metal bowl to
become quite hot, and then put into it—half pint of brandy; half
pint of rum; quarter of a pound of lump sugar; the juice of a large
lemon. Set these a light and pour in the tea gradually, mixing it
from time to time with a ladle. It will remain burning for some
time, and is to be poured in that state into the glasses. In order
to increase the flavour a few lumps of the sugar should be rubbed
over the lemon peel. This punch may be made in a china bowl,
but in that case the flame goes off more rapidly.

50   WEST INDIA PUNCH.

This punch is made the same as Brandy Punch (No. 1), but to
each glass add one clove or two small pieces of preserved ginger
with a little of its syrup.

51   BARBADOES PUNCH.

To each glass of Brandy Punch (No. 1) add a tea-spoonful of
Guava Jelly.

52   APPLE PUNCH.

Place in a china bowl slices of apples and lemons alternately, each layer being thickly strewn with powdered sugar. Pour over the fruit, when the bowl is half filled, a bottle of claret ; cover, and let it stand six hours ; then pour it through a muslin bag and serve immediately.

53   ALE PUNCH.

A quart of Burton ale; a glass of Neirsteiner wine ; one wine glass of brandy ; one of Cappilaire (see No. 46) ; the juice of a lemon ; a roll of the peel pared thin; grated nutmeg on the top and a slice of toasted bread.

54   CIDER PUNCH.

On the thin rind of a lemon pour half a pint of sherry ; add a quarter of a pound of sugar, the juice of a lemon, a little grated nutmeg, and a bottle of cider. Mix it well, and if possible place it in ice. Add, before served, a glass of brandy and a few pieces of cucumber peel.

55   NECTAR PUNCH.

Infuse the peel of fifteen lemons in a pint and a half of rum for forty-eight hours; add two quarts of cold water with three quarts of rum (exclusive of the former pint and a half); also the juice of the lemons with two quarts of boiling milk and one grated nutmeg. Let it stand for twenty-four hours covered close. Add two pounds and a half of loaf sugar ; then strain it through a flannel bag till quite fine, and bottle for use. It is fit for use as soon as bottled.

EGG NOGG.

————:o:————

Egg Nogg is a beverage of American origin, and has gained a popularity all over the world. In the South it is almost indispensable at Christmas time, in the East the wise men imbibe it, in the West the egotist believes in it, and in the North it is a favourite at all seasons. In Scotland, Egg Nogg is known by the name of "Auld Man's milk."

56   EGG NOGG.
Use large tumbler.

One table-spoonful of fine sugar, dissolved with one table-spoonful of cold water ; one egg ; one wine glass of Cognac ; half a wine glass of Santa Cruz rum or Jamaica rum ; a quarter of a tumbler of shaved ice, fill up with milk, shake the ingredients until they are thoroughly mixed together, and grate a little nutmeg on the top.

57   HOT EGG NOGG.

This drink is very popular in England, and is made in precisely the same manner as the cold Egg Nogg above, except that you must use boiling water instead of ice.

58   EGG NOGG.
For a Party of Ten.

Three eggs ; one pint of brandy ; two and a half wine glasses of Santa Cruz rum ; two quarts of milk ; six ounces of white sugar. Separate the whites of the eggs from the yolks, beat them separately with an egg-beater until the yolks are well cut up, and the whites assume a light fleecy appearance. Mix all the ingredients (except the whites of the eggs) in a large punch-bowl, then let the whites float on the top, and ornament with coloured sugars. Cool in a tub of ice, and serve.

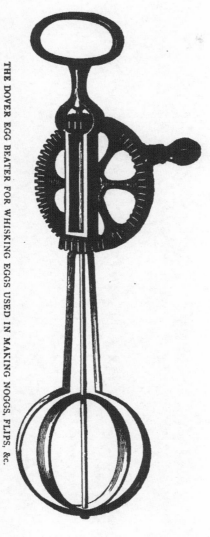

THE DOVER EGG BEATER FOR WHISKING EGGS USED IN MAKING NOGGS, FLIPS, &c.

59   BALTIMORE EGG NOGG.

For a Party of Fifteen.

Take the yolks of sixteen eggs, and twelve table-spoonfuls of powdered loaf sugar, and beat them to the consistency of cream; to this add two-thirds of a nutmeg grated, and beat them together; then mix in half a pint of brandy or Jamaica rum, and two wine glasses of Madeira. Have ready the whites of the eggs whipped to a stiff froth, which then beat into the mixture. When this is done, stir in six pints of rich milk. There is no heat used. Egg Nogg made in this manner is digestible, and will not cause headache. It makes an excellent drink for debilitated persons and a nourishing diet for consumptives.

60 GENERAL HARRISON'S EGG NOGG.

Use large tumbler.

One egg; one and a half tea-spoonful of sugar; two or three small lumps of ice. Fill the tumbler with cider and shake well. This is a splendid drink, and is very popular on the Mississippi river. It was General Harrison's favourite drink.

61   SHERRY EGG NOGG.

One table-spoonful of white sugar; one egg; two wine glasses of sherry. Dissolve the sugar with a little water; break the yolk of an egg in a large glass; put in one quarter of a tumbler of broken ice; fill with milk, and shake up until the egg is thoroughly mixed with the other ingredients; then grate a little nutmeg on top, and *" Quaff the nectar cup, which gives delight."*

JULEPS.

—:o:—

THE Julep is peculiarly an American beverage, and in the Southern States is more popular than in any other. It was first introduced into England by Captain Marryatt, where it is now quite a favourite. The gallant Captain appears to have been a great patroniser of this drink, and published the recipe in his work on America. We give it in his own words:—"I must descant a little upon the mint julep, as it is, with the thermometer at 100^0, one of the most delightful and insinuating potations that ever was invented, and may be drunk with equal satisfaction when the thermometer is at 70^0. There are many varieties, such as those composed of claret, Madeira, &c., &c., but the ingredients of the real Mint Julep are as follow; I learnt how to make them and succeeded pretty well:—Put into a tumbler about a dozen sprigs of the tender shoots of mint; upon them put a spoonful of white sugar and equal proportions of peach and common brandy, so as to fill it up one-third, or perhaps a little less; then take rasped or powdered ice and fill up the tumbler. Epicures rub the lips of the tumbler with a piece of fresh pine-apple, and the tumbler itself is very often incrusted outside with stalactites of ice. As the ice melts you drink. I once overheard two ladies talking in the next room to me, and one of them said: 'Well, if I have a weakness for any one thing, it is for a mint julep.' A very amiable weakness, and proving her good sense and good taste. They are, in fact, like the American ladies, irresistable."

BUNDLE OF STRAWS USED IN SIPPING COBBLERS JULEPS, &c.

62   ## MINT JULEP.
Use large tumbler.

One table-spoonful of powdered sugar ; two table-spoonfuls of
water ; mix well with a spoon ; take three or four sprigs of fresh
mint and press them well in the sugar and water until the flavour
of the mint is extracted ; add one and a half wine glass of Cognac,
and fill the glass with fine chipped ice ; then draw out the sprigs
of mint and insert them in the ice with the stems downward,
so that the leaves will be above in the shape of a bouquet. Arrange
berries and small pieces of sliced orange on top in a tasteful manner ;
dash with Jamaica rum, and sprinkle white sugar on top. Sip
through a straw, and you have a julep fit for an Emperor.

63   ## BRANDY JULEP.
Use large tumbler.

The Brandy Julep is made with the same ingredients as the Mint
Julep, omitting the fancy *fixings*.

64   ## GIN JULEP.
Use large tumbler.

The Gin Julep is made with the same ingredients as the Mint
Julep, omitting the fancy *fixings*, and substituting gin for brandy.

65   ## WHISKEY JULEP.
Use large tumbler.

The Whiskey Julep is made the same as the Mint Julep, omitting
all fruits and berries, and substituting whiskey for brandy.

66   ## PINE-APPLE JULEP.
For a Party of Five.

Peel, slice, and cut up a ripe pine-apple into a glass bowl ; add
the juice of two oranges ; a gill of raspberry syrup ; a gill of
Maraschino ; a gill of old gin ; a bottle of sparkling Moselle, and
about a pound of pure shaved ice. Mix, ornament with berries
in season, and serve in tumblers.

THE SMASH.

———:o:———

THIS beverage is a Julep on a small scale.

67   BRANDY SMASH.

Use small tumbler.

Half a table-spoonful of white sugar ; one table-spoonful of water ; one wine glass of brandy. Fill two-thirds full of shaved ice. Use several sprigs of mint, the same as in the recipe for Mint Julep. Place two small pieces of orange on top, and ornament with berries in season.

68   GIN SMASH.

Use small tumbler.

Half a table-spoonful of white sugar ; one table-spoonful of water ; one wine glass of gin. Fill two-thirds full of chipped ice. Use two sprigs of mint, the same as in the recipe for Mint Julep. Lay two small pieces of orange on top, and ornament with berries in season.

69   WHISKEY SMASH.

Use small tumbler.

Half a table-spoonful of white sugar ; one table-spoonful of water ; one wine glass of Bourbon whiskey. Fill two-thirds full of shaved ice, and use two sprigs of mint, the same as in the recipe for Mint Julep.

SMASHES SHOULD BE DRANK THROUGH A STRAINER, BUT
WHEN THAT IS NOT TO HAND, A MOUSTACHE CUP,
AS PER CUT, WILL ANSWER THE PURPOSE.

COBBLERS.

——:o:——

THIS charming potation is an American invention, and has become a great favourite in all warm climates. The Cobbler is now a popular drink with both patrician and plebeian, and requires but very little skill in compounding. But to make it acceptable to the eye as well as to the palate, it is necessary to display a certain degree of taste in dressing the glass after the beverage is made.

70 SHERRY COBBLER.
Use large tumbler.

Two wine glasses of sherry ; one table-spoonful of sugar ; two or three slices of orange. Fill a tumbler with shaved ice, shake well, and ornament with berries in season. Dash with port wine. Drink through a straw.

71 CHAMPAGNE COBBLER.
One Bottle of Champagne to four Goblets.

One table-spoonful of sugar ; one piece each of orange and lemon-peel. Fill the tumbler one-third full with ice, and fill balance with Champagne. Ornament in a tasty manner with berries in season. This beverage should be sipped through a straw.

72   CATAWBA COBBLER.

Use large tumbler.

One tea-spoonful of sugar dissolved in one table-spoonful of water ;
two wine glasses of Catawba. Fill the tumbler with chipped ice, and
ornament with sliced oranges and berries in season. Sip through
a straw.

73   HOCK COBBLER.

Use large tumbler.

This drink is made in the same way as No. 72, using Hock
instead of Catawba.

74   CLARET COBBLER.

Use large tumbler.

This drink is made in the same way as No. 72, using Claret
instead of Catawba.

75   SAUTERNE COBBLER.

Use large tumbler.

The same as No. 72, using Sauterne instead of Catawba.

76   WHISKEY COBBLER.

Use large tumbler.

Two wine glasses of whiskey ; one table-spoonful of sugar ; two
or three slices of orange. Fill tumbler with ice, and shake well.
Imbibe through a straw.

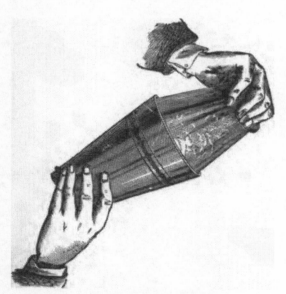

MODE OF SHAKING OR MIXING A COBBLER, &c.

THE COCKTAIL AND CRUSTA.

————:o:————

THE Cocktail is quite a modern invention, and is very frequently used as the "proper beverage" for fishing and other sporting parties, although we have heard of some "weary sufferers" who take it in the morning as a tonic. The Crusta is thought by some to be an improvement on the Cocktail, and is said to have been invented by Santina, a celebrated Spanish caterer.

77   CRITERION COCKTAIL.

To make a splendid bottle of Criterion Cocktail, use the following ingredients :—Three-eighths of a bottle of brandy ; half a pint of water ; one liqueur glass of Boker's bitters ; one wine glass of plain syrup ; half a liqueur glass of Benedictine. The author has always used this recipe in compounding the above beverage for connoisseurs. Whiskey and Gin Cocktails in bottles may be made by using the above recipe, substituting those liquors in place of brandy.

78   BRANDY COCKTAIL.

Use small tumbler.

Three dashes of plain syrup ; two or three dashes of bitters (Boker's) ; one wine glass of brandy ; one or two dashes of orange Curaçoa. Squeeze lemon peel, fill one-third full of ice, and stir with a spoon.

79   FANCY BRANDY COCKTAIL.

Use small tumbler.

This drink is made the same as the Criterion Cocktail, except that it is strained into a fancy wine glass, and a piece of lemon peel thrown on top, and the edge of the glass moistened with lemon and dipped in sugar.

80   WHISKEY COCKTAIL.

Use small tumbler.

Three dashes of plain syrup ; two or three dashes of bitters, as above ; one wine glass of Bourbon or Rye whiskey, and a piece of lemon peel. Fill one-third full of fine ice, shake, and strain in a fancy white wine glass.

81   CHAMPAGNE COCKTAIL.

Half a tea-spoonful of sugar ; one or two dashes of bitters ; one piece of lemon peel. Fill tumbler one-third full of broken ice, and fill balance with Champagne.   Use strainer.

82   GIN COCKTAIL.

Use small tumbler.

Three dashes of plain syrup ; two or three dashes of bitters (Boker's); one wine glass of Hollands or gin ; one or two dashes of orange Curaçoa. Squeeze lemon peel. Fill one-third full of ice, and shake well, and strain in a glass.

83   **FANCY COCKTAIL.**

Use small tumbler.

This drink is made the same way as the Gin Cocktail, except that it is strained in a fancy wine glass and a piece of lemon peel thrown on top; the edge of the glass moistened with lemon, and dipped in white or coloured sugar.

84   **JAPANESE COCKTAIL.**

Use small tumbler.

One table-spoonful of Orgeat syrup; half a tea-spoonful of bitters; one wine glass of brandy; one or two pieces of lemon peel. Fill the tumbler one-third with ice, and stir well with a spoon.

85   **JERSEY COCKTAIL.**

Use small tumbler.

One tea-spoonful of sugar; two dashes of bitters. Fill tumbler with cider, and mix well; serve with lemon peel on the top.

86   **SODA COCKTAIL.**

Use large tumbler.

The same as No. 85, using soda-water instead of cider.

87   **BRANDY CRUSTA.**

Use small tumbler.

Crusta is made the same way as a Fancy Cocktail, with a little lemon juice and a small lump of ice added. First mix the ingredients in a small tumbler, then take a fancy red wine glass, put a sliced lemon round the rim of the glass, and dip it in powdered white sugar, so that the sugar will adhere to the edge of the glass; pare half a lemon, the same as you would an apple (all in one piece), so that the paring will fit into the wine glass, and strain Crusta from the tumbler into it.

88   WHISKEY CRUSTA.

Use small tumbler.

The Whiskey Crusta is made the same as the Brandy Crusta, using whiskey instead of brandy.

89   GIN CRUSTA.

Use small tumbler.

Gin Crusta is made the same as Brandy Crusta, using gin instead of brandy.

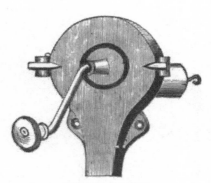

NUTMEG GRATER.

MULLS AND SANGAREES.

————:o:————

MULLED WINE.

To make good Mulled Wine, just allow me to say—
Nine eggs you must break, and then do not delay,
But into a bowl let the whites all be dropped,
Whilst all of the yolks in another are popped.
With a switch let the whites be beaten about
Until like the froth of the sea they come out;
To the yolks then attend, and beat them also,
And at them three spoonfuls of sugar just throw.
Now into a skillet it's quite time to pour
Of some recognised brand a bottle or more ;
And if of your head you may have any fear,
Add one pint of water, and mind it is clear.
The water and wine must be kept on the fire
Till they reach the boiling heat you require;
Then the yolks and the whites please beat as before,
A half pint of water o'er them gently pour.
Mix all well together until they combine,
And then turn them into the skillet of wine;
Stir about briskly and pour in a pitcher,
Add grated nutmeg, 'twill make it much richer.
Drink it off hot, and I'll bet any odds
You'll own it's a drink that is fit for the gods.

91   MULLED WINE.

Another.

Dissolve one pound of sugar in two pints of hot water, to which add two and a half pints of good sherry, let the mixture be set upon the fire until it almost boils ; meantime beat up the whites of twelve eggs to a froth, and pour into them the hot mixture, stirring rapidly. Add a little nutmeg.

92   MULLED WINE, WITH EGGS.

One quart of wine ; one pint of water ; one table-spoonful of allspice, and nutmeg to taste. Boil them together a few minutes ; beat up six eggs, with sugar to taste ; pour the boiling wine on the eggs, stirring it all the time. Be careful not to pour the eggs into the wine or they will curdle.

93   MULLED WINE, WITHOUT EGGS.

To every pint of wine allow one small tumbler of water ; sugar and spice to taste. In making preparations like the above, it is very difficult to give the exact proportions of ingredients like sugar and spice, as what quantity might suit one person would be to another quite distasteful. Boil the spice in the water until the flavour is extracted, then add the wine and sugar, and bring the whole to the boiling point ; then serve with strips of dry toast, or with biscuits. The spices usually used for Mulled Wine are cloves, grated nutmeg, cinnamon or mace. Any kind of wine may be mulled, but port or claret are those usually selected for the purpose, and the latter requires a larger proportion of sugar.

94   MULLED CLARET.

The same as No. 91, using claret instead of sherry.

95 PORT WINE SANGAREE.

Use large tumbler.

One and a half wine glass of port wine ; one tea-spoonful of sugar. Fill tumbler two-thirds with ice ; shake well, and grate nutmeg on top, and place slices of lemon on the inside of glass.

96 SHERRY SANGAREE.

Use large tumbler.

One wine glass of sherry; one tea-spoonful of fine sugar. Fill tumbler one-third with ice, shake, and grate nutmeg on top.

97 BRANDY SANGAREE.

Use large tumbler.

The Brandy Sangaree is made with the same ingredients as the Brandy Toddy (see No. 102), omitting the nutmeg. Fill two-thirds with ice, and dash about a tea-spoonful of port wine, so that it may float on top.

98 GIN SANGAREE.

The Gin Sangaree is made with the same ingredients as the Gin Toddy (see No. 104), omitting the nutmeg. Fill two-thirds with ice, and dash about a tea-spoonful of port wine, so that it may float on top.

99 ALE SANGAREE.

Use small tumbler.

One tea-spoonful of sugar dissolved in a tea-spoonful of water. Fill the tumbler with ale, and grate nutmeg on the top.

100 PORTER SANGAREE.

This beverage is made the same as Ale Sangaree, and is sometimes called Porteree.

TODDIES AND SLINGS.

————:o:————

THESE drinks are greatly patronized in all countries.

101   APPLE TODDY.
Use small tumbler.

One table-spoonful of fine white sugar; one wine glass of cider brandy (Apple Jack); half of a baked apple. Fill the glass two-thirds full of boiling water, and grate a little nutmeg on top.

102   BRANDY TODDY.
Use small tumbler.

One tea-spoonful of sugar; half a wine glass of water; one wine glass of brandy; one small lump of ice. Stir with a spoon. For hot Brandy Toddy omit the ice, and use boiling water.

103   WHISKEY TODDY.
Use small tumbler.

One tea-spoonful of sugar; half a wine glass of water; one wine glass of whiskey; one small lump of ice. Stir with a spoon.

104   GIN TODDY.
Use small tumbler.

One tea-spoonful of sugar; half a wine glass of water; one wine glass of gin; one small lump of ice. Stir with a spoon.

105 SLING

Use small tumbler.

The Gin Sling is made with the same ingredients as the Gin Toddy, adding a little grated nutmeg on top.

106 HOT WHISKEY SLING.

Use small tumbler.

One wine glass of whiskey. Fill tumbler one-third full of boiling water, and grate nutmeg on the top.

FIXES AND SOURS.

————:o:————

THESE drinks have become established favourites with the present generation.

107 BRANDY FIX.

Use small tumbler.

One table-spoonful of sugar ; half a wine glass of water ; quarter of a lemon ; one wine glass of brandy. Fill the tumbler two-thirds full of ice, stir with a spoon, and ornament the top with fruits in season.

108 GIN FIX.

Use small tumbler.

One table-spoonful of sugar ; half a wine glass of water ; quarter of a lemon ; one wine glass of gin. Fill two-thirds full of ice, stir with a spoon, and ornament the top with fruits in season.

109 BRANDY SOUR.

Use small tumbler.

The Brandy Sour is made with the same ingredients as the Brandy Fix, omitting all fruits, except a small piece of lemon, the juice of which must be pressed into the glass.

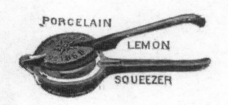

110   GIN SOUR.

Use small tumbler.

The Gin Sour is made with the same ingredients as the Gin Fix,
omitting all fruits, except a small piece of lemon, the juice of which
must be pressed into the glass.

111   SANTA CRUZ FIX.

Use small tumbler.

Is made by substituting Santa Cruz rum instead of other spirits.

Note.—In making Fixes and Sours, be careful to put the lemon
skin in the glass.

114   ALE FLIP.

Put on the fire, in a saucepan, one quart of ale, and let it boil ; have ready the whites of two eggs and the yolks of four, well beaten up separately ; add them by degrees to four table-spoonfuls of moist sugar and half a nutmeg, grated. When all are well mixed, pour on the boiling ale by degrees, beating up the mixture continually, then pour it rapidly backwards and forwards from one jug to another, keeping one jug raised high above the other, till the flip is smooth and finely frothed. This is a good and *delightful* remedy for a cold.

115   EGG FLIP.

Put a quart of ale in a saucepan on the fire to boil. In the meantime, beat up the yolks of four eggs with the whites of two, adding four table-spoonfuls of brown sugar and a little nutmeg. Pour on the ale by degrees, beating up so as to prevent the mixture from curdling; then pour backwards and forwards repeatedly from vessel to vessel, raising the hand to as great a height as possible, which process produces the smoothness and frothing essential to the good quality of flip. This is excellent for a cold; and, from its fleecy appearance, is sometimes designated "a yard of flannel."

116   EGG FLIP.

Another way.

Beat up in a jug four new-laid eggs, omitting two of the whites; add half a dozen lumps of sugar, and rub these well in the eggs. Pour in boiling water, about half a pint at a time; and when the jug is nearly full, throw in two wine glasses of Cognac brandy and one wine glass of old Jamaica rum.

117   BRANDY FLIP.

Use small tumbler.

One tea-spoonful of sugar; one wine glass of brandy. Fill the tumbler one-third full of hot water; mix, and place a toasted biscuit or pulled bread on top, and grate nutmeg on it.

118   PORT WINE NEGUS.

To every pint of port allow one quart of boiling water; quarter of a pound of loaf sugar; one lemon; grated nutmeg to taste. Put the wine in a jug; rub some lumps of sugar (a quarter of a pound) on the lemon rind until all the yellow part of the skin is absorbed; then squeeze the juice and strain it; add the sugar and lemon juice to the port wine, with the grated nutmeg; pour on the boiling water, cover the jug, and when the beverage has cooled a little, it will be ready for use. Negus may also be made of sherry or any other sweet wine, but it is more usually made of port. This beverage derives its name from Colonel Negus, who is said to have invented it.

119   PORT WINE NEGUS.

(Another.)

Use small tumbler.

One wine glass of port wine; one tea-spoonful of sugar. Fill tumbler one-third full with hot water. Grated nutmeg on top.

120   SODA NEGUS.

A most refreshing and elegant beverage, particularly for those who do not take punch or grog at night :—Put half a pint of port wine, with four lumps of sugar, three cloves, and enough grated nutmeg to cover a shilling, into a saucepan; warm it well, but do not allow it to boil. Pour it into a bowl or jug, and, upon the warm wine, decant a bottle of soda-water. You will have a delicious and effervescing negus by this means.

FANCY DRINKS.

——:o:——

WE have heard of somebody having exclaimed, "Tell me where is
Fancy bred." We can now confidently answer that question—in
England, France, Germany, Russia, Italy, Spain, and America;
and as a guarantee for our knowledge, we give the following
recipes for Fancy Drinks:—

121   SANTINA'S POUSÉE CAFÉ.

Use small Taper Wine Glass.

This delicious drink is made from a recipe by Santina, proprietor
of Santina's Saloons, a celebrated French Café, in New Orleans.—
One-third brandy ; one-third Maraschino ; one-third Curaçoa, each
to be poured in gently at the side of the glass, so that neither
mixes with the other.

122   PARISIAN POUSÉE CAFÉ.

Use small Taper Wine Glass.

Two-fifths orange Curaçoa; two-fifths Kirschenwasser; one-fifth
green Chartreuse. Pour into the glass as in No. 121.

123   FAIVRE'S POUSÉE CAFÉ.

Use small Taper Wine Glass.

One-third Parisian Pousée Café (No. 122); one-third Kirsch-
wasser; one-third Curaçoa. This celebrated drink is from a recipe
of M. Faivre, a popular proprietor of a French Saloon in New York

124   POUSÉE L'AMOUR.

To mix this, fill a wine glass half full of Maraschino; then put in the pure yolk of an egg. Surround the yolk with Vanilla cordial, and dash the top with Cognac.

125   BRANDY CHAMPERELLE.

Use Wine Glass.

One-third brandy; one-third Angostura bitters; one-third Curaçoa. This is a delicious French Café drink.

126   BRANDY SCAFFA.

Use Wine Glass.

One-half brandy; one-half Maraschino; two dashes of bitters.

127 CLARET OR CHAMPAGNE CUP.

These drinks are highly appreciated in Russia, where for many years they have enjoyed a high reputation amongst the aristocracy of the Muscovite's Empire. Proportions:—Three bottles of claret; two-thirds of a pint of Curaçoa; one pint of sherry; half-pint of brandy; two wine glasses of syrup of raspberries; three oranges, and one lemon cut in slices; some sprigs of borage; a small piece of rind of cucumber; two bottles of German seltzer; three bottles of soda-water. Stir this together, and sweeten with Capillaire or pounded sugar until it ferments. Let it stand one hour; strain it and ice it well, it is then ready for use. Serve in small glasses. The same for Champagne Cup—Champagne instead of claret; Noyeau instead of raspberry.

128   SLEEPER.

To a gill of old rum add one ounce of sugar; two yolks of eggs; the juice of half a lemon. Boil half a pint of water with six cloves, six coriander seeds, and a bit of cinnamon. Whisk all together and strain them into a tumbler.

129   RUSSIAN AMBROSIAL FLUID.

For a Party of Fifteen.

Thinly peel the rind of half a lemon, shred it fine, and put it in a punch bowl; add two table-spoonfuls of crushed sugar, and the juice of two lemons; the half of a small cucumber sliced thin with the peel on. Toss it up several times, then add two bottles of soda-water; two bottles of claret, or one of Champagne. Stir well together and serve.

130   WHITE LION.

One and a half tea-spoonful of powdered white sugar; half a lime (squeeze out juice and put the rind in glass)—one wine glass of Santa; Cruz rum; half a tea-spoonful of Curaçoa; half a tea-spoonful of raspbery syrup. Mix well, ornament with berries in season, and cool with chipped ice.

131   CRIMEAN CUP.

For a Party of Thirty.

One quart of syrup of oranges; one pint Otard brandy; half a pint of Maraschino; half a pint of Jamaica rum; two bottles of Champagne; two bottles of soda-water; six ounces of sugar; four medium sized lemons. Thinly peel the lemons, and place the rind in a bowl with the sugar. Macerate them well for a minute or two in order to extract the flavour from the lemons; next squeeze the juice of the lemons upon this, add two bottles of soda-water, and stir well till the sugar is dissolved; pour in the syrup of oranges and whip the mixture well with an egg whisk, in order to whiten the composition; then add the brandy, rum and Maraschino. Strain the whole into a punch bowl and, just before serving, add the champagne, which should be well iced. While adding the champagne stir well with ladle, this will render the Cup creamy and mellow.

132   CRIMEAN CUP (A la Wyndham.)
For a Party of Five.

Thinly peel the rind of half an orange, put it into a bowl with a table-spoonful of crushed sugar, and macerate with the ladle for a minute or two; then add one wine glass of Maraschino; half a wine glass of Cognac; the same of Curaçoa. Mix well together; pour in two bottles of soda-water, and one of Champagne, during which time work it up and down with the punch ladle, and it is ready. A pound of pure ice is a great improvement.

133   TOM AND JERRY.
Use Punch-bowl for this mixture.

Five pounds of powdered sugar; twelve eggs; half a small glass of Jamaica rum; one and a half tea-spoonful of ground cinnamon; half a tea-spoonful of ground cloves; half a tea-spoonful of all-spice. Beat the white of the eggs to a stiff froth, and the yolks until they are as thin as water, then mix together and add spice and rum. Thicken with sugar until the mixture attains the consistency of a light batter.

TO SERVE OUT TOM AND JERRY.

Take a tumbler, and to one table-spoonful of the above mixture add one wine glass of brandy, and fill the glass with boiling water; stir with a spoon, and grate a little nutmeg on top. Adepts in serving Tom and Jerry sometimes adopt a mixture of half brandy, quarter Jamaica rum, and quarter Santa Cruz rum, instead of brandy plain. This compound is usually mixed and kept in a bottle, and a wine glass full is used to each tumbler of Tom and Jerry.

134   LOCOMOTIVE.

Put two yolks of eggs into a goblet, with an ounce of honey, a little essence of cloves, and a liqueur glass of Curaçoa. Add a pint of high Burgundy made hot. Whisk well together and serve hot in glasses.

135 BISHOP.

Stick an orange full of cloves and roast it before the fire ; when brown cut it in quarters and pour over it a quart of hot port wine ; add sugar to taste. Let mixture simmer for half an hour.

136 ARCHBISHOP.

The same as Bishop, substituting claret for the port.

137 CARDINAL.

Same as above, substituting Champagne for claret.

138 POPE.

Same as above, substituting Burgundy for Champagne.

139 A BISHOP (Protestant).

Four table-spoonfuls of white sugar; two tumblers of water; one lemon in slices; one bottle of claret; four table-spoonfuls of Santa Cruz rum; ice.

140 KNICKERBOCKER.

Use small tumbler.

Half a lime or lemon, squeeze out the juice and put rind and juice in the glass; two tea-spoonfuls of raspberry syrup; one wine glass of Santa Cruz rum; half tea-spoonful of Curaçoa. Cool with chipped ice, shake up well, and ornament with berries in season. If this be not sweet enough, put in a little more raspberry syrup.

141   RUMFUSTIAN.

Let the yolks of a dozen eggs be well whisked up and put into a quart of strong beer; to this add a pint of gin. Put a bottle of sherry into a saucepan, with a stick of cinnamon, a nutmeg grated, a dozen large lumps of sugar, and the rind of a lemon peeled very thin. When the wine boils it is poured upon the gin and beer, and is drunk hot.

142   CLARET CUP.

To a bottle of thin claret add half a pint of cold water, a table-spoonful of powdered sugar, and a tea-spoonful of cinnamon, cloves, and all-spice finely powdered and mixed together. Mix all well together, and add half the thin rind of a small lemon. This is a delicious summer beverage for evening parties.

143   PORTER CUP.

Mix, in a tankard or covered jug, a bottle of porter, and an equal quantity of table-beer; pour in a glass of brandy, a dessert-spoonful of syrup of ginger; add three or four lumps of sugar and half a nutmeg grated. Cover it down and expose it to the cold for half an hour. Just before sending it to table, stir in a tea-spoonfu of carbonate of soda, and add the fresh cut rind of a cucumber.

144   ITALIAN LEMONADE.

Pare and press twenty-four lemons; pour the juice on the peels and let it remain on them all night. In the morning add two pounds of loaf sugar, a quart of good sherry, and three quarts of boiling water. Mix well; add a quart of boiling milk, and strain it through a jelly bag until clear.

145 CLARET CUP, or MULLED CLARET.

Peel one lemon; add to it some white powdered sugar; pour over one glass of sherry; then add a bottle of Bordeaux, and sweeten to taste. One bottle of soda-water, and nutmeg if you like it. For Cup, strain and ice it well; for Mull, heat it and serve it hot.

146 BOTTLED SILK.

A bottle of Moselle; half a pint of sherry; the peel of a lemon not too much, so as to have the flavour predominate; two table-spoonfuls of sugar, and a sprig of Verbena. All must be well mixed, and then strained and iced.

147 CHAMPAGNE, HOCK, or CHABLIS CUP.

Dissolve four or five lumps of sugar in a quarter of a pint of boiling water, with a little very thin lemon peel; let it stand a quarter of an hour; add one bottle of the above wines and a sprig of Verbena; a small glass of sherry; half a pint of water. Mix well and let it stand half an hour. Strain and ice it well.

148 CIDER NECTAR, (a la Ritchie.)

One quart of cider; one bottle of soda water; one glass of sherry; one wine glass of brandy; juice of half a lemon; peel of a quarter of a lemon; sugar and nutmeg to taste; a spring of Verbena. Flavour it to taste with pine-apple. Strain and ice it all well. This is a very delicious beverage.

149 BADMINTON.

Peel half of a medium-sized cucumber, and put it into a silver cup, with four ounces of powdered sugar, a little nutmeg, and a bottle of claret. When the sugar is thoroughly dissolved, pour in a bottle of soda-water, and it is fit for use.

150   BLUE BLAZER.

Use two large silver plated Mugs with handles.

One wine glass of Scotch whiskey ; one wine glass of boiling water. Put the whiskey and boiling water in one mug, ignite the liquid, and while blazing mix both ingredients by pouring them four or five times from one mug to the other. If well done, this will have the appearance of a continued stream of fire. Sweeten with one tea-spoonful of powdered white sugar, and serve in a small tumbler, with a piece of lemon.

151   BURNT BRANDY AND PEACH.

Use small tumbler.

This drink is very popular in the Southern States, where it is sometimes used as a cure for diarrhœa. One wine glass of Cognac ; half a table-spoonful of white sugar ; two or three slices of dried peach. Place the dried fruit in a glass, and pour the liquid over them.

152   BLACK STRIPE.

Use small tumbler.

One wine glass of Santa Cruz rum ; one table-spoonful of molasses. This drink can either be made in summer or winter. If in the former season, mix in one table-spoonful of water, and cool with chipped ice ; if in the latter, fill up the tumbler with boiling water. Grate a little nutmeg on top in either case.

153   PEACH AND HONEY.

Use small tumbler.

A table-spoonful of honey ; a wine glass of peach brandy. Stir with a spoon.

154   GIN AND PINE.
Use Wine Glass.

Split the heart of a green pine log into fine splints, about the size of a cedar lead pencil, take two ounces of the same, and put into a quart decanter, and fill the decanter with gin. Let the pine soak for two hours, and the gin will be ready to serve.

155   GIN AND TANSY.
Use Wine Glass.

Fill a quart decanter one-third full of tansy, and pour in gin to fill up.

156   GIN AND WORMWOOD.

Put three or four sprigs of wormwood into a quart decanter, and fill up with gin.

157   SCOTCH WHISKEY SKIN.

One wine glass Scotch whiskey ; one piece of lemon peel. Fill the tumbler one-half full with boiling water.

158   HOT SPICED RUM.
Use small tumbler.

One tea-spoonful of sugar ; one wine glass of Jamaica rum ; one tea-spoonful of mixed spices ; a piece of butter as large as a chestnut. Fill the tumbler with hot water.

159   STONE FENCE.

One wine glass of whiskey (Bourbon) ; two or three lumps of ice. Fill up the glass with sweet cider.

160   RHINE RELISH.

Fill large tumbler half full of Rhine wine, and fill up with soda water.

TEMPERANCE DRINKS.

——:o:——

"To be merry and wise" is a very good motto, and should be ever in our mind. We know perfectly well that in hot weather ardent spirits absorb and assimulate all the liquid that is left in the fevered frame, and it is to be regretted that in England there is no common use of such a harmless mixture as orgeat, or those pleasant, innocent beverages with which the Italians, in their cool arcades, consume long hours. When people are very hot they will drink, and the discussion of the subject may help to make drinks more wholesome. The simple use of the lemon, with really pure ice, is the one good which America has given us. We say the use of the lemon instead of lemonade, because cheap lemonade is often a mixture of impure water and chemical acid. The best thing of all for preventing the ills of hot weather is probably to abstain altogether from any iced drinks ; but, in the opinion of the thirsty, the remedy would be worse than the disease.—*From the Globe newspaper.*

161   LEMONADE.
                  Use large tumbler.

The juice of half a lemon ; one and a half table-spoonful of sugar ; two or three pieces of orange ; one table-spoonful of raspberry or strawberry syrup. Fill the tumbler half full of chipped ice, the balance with water. Dash with port wine, and ornament with fruits in season.

162 PLAIN LEMONADE.
From a recipe by the celebrated Soyer.

Cut in very thin slices, three lemons, put them in a basin; add half a pound of sugar (either white or brown); bruise all together. Add a gallon of water, and stir well.

163 LEMONADE.
For Parties.

The rind of two lemons ; juice of three large lemons ; half pound of loaf sugar ; one quart boiling water. Rub some of the sugar in lumps on two of the lemons, until they have imbibed all the oil from them, and put it with the remainder of the sugar into a jug; add the lemon juice, and pour over the whole a quart of boiling water. When the sugar is dissolved, strain the lemonade through a piece of muslin, and when cool it will be ready for use. The lemonade will be much improved by having the white of an egg beaten up in it. A little sherry mixed with it also makes this beverage much nicer.

164 ORANGEADE.

This agreeable beverage is made the same way as lemonade, substituting oranges for lemons.

165 ORGEAT LEMONADE.
Use large tumbler.

Half a wine glass of orgeat syrup ; the juice of half a lemon. Fill the tumbler one-third full of ice, and then fill up with water. Shake well, and ornament with berries in season.

166 DRINK FOR THE DOG DAYS.

A bottle of soda-water poured into a large goblet in which a lemon ice has been placed, forms a deliciously cool and refreshing drink, but should be taken with some care, and positively avoided whilst you are very hot.

167   SODA NECTAR.

Use large tumbler.

The juice of one lemon ; three quarters of a tumblerful of water ; powdered white sugar to taste ; half a tea-spoonful of carbonate of soda. Strain the juice of the lemon and add it to the water, with sufficient white sugar to sweeten the whole nicely. When well mixed, put in the soda, stir well, and drink while the mixture is in an effervescing state.

168   SHERBET.

Eight ounces of carbonate of soda ; six ounces of tartaric acid ; two pounds of loaf sugar (finely powdered) ; three drachms of essence of lemon. Let the powder be very dry. Mix thoroughly, and keep them for use in a wide-mouthed bottle closely corked. Put two good-sized tea-spoonfuls into a tumbler, pour in half a pint of cold water, stir briskly, and drink off.

169   LEMONADE POWDERS.

One pound of finely-powdered loaf sugar, one ounce of tartaric or citric acid, and twenty drops of essence of lemon. Mix, and keep very dry. Two or three tea-spoonfuls of this stirred briskly in a tumbler of water will make a very pleasant glass of lemonade. If effervescent lemonade be desired, one ounce of carbonate of soda must be added to the mixture.

170   GINGER-BEER POWDERS.

Two drachms powdered white sugar ; five grains powdered ginger ; twenty-six grains carbonate of soda ; mix. Dissolve in half a glass of spring water, and drink while in a state of effervescence.

AMERICAN ICED WATER PITCHER

171   LEMON SHERBET.

One ounce of cream of tartar, one ounce of tartaric or citric acid, the juice and peel of two lemons, and half a pound or more of loaf sugar. The sweetening must be regulated according to taste.

172   DRINK FOR HOME.

Two ounces of cream of tartar, the juice and peel of two or three lemons, and half a pound of coarse sugar. Put these into a gallon pitcher, and pour on boiling water. When cool, it will be fit for use.

173   NECTAR.

One drachm of citric acid ; one scruple of bicarbonate of potash ; one ounce of white sugar, powdered. Fill a soda-water bottle nearly full of water, drop in the potash and sugar, and lastly the citric acid, cork the bottle up immediately, and shake. As soon as the crystals are dissolved, the nectar is fit for use. It may be coloured with a small portion of cochineal.

174   ORANGE SHERBET.

One pound of pounded sugar ; two drops of neroli ; four drops of essence of orange peel ; half an ounce of citric acid. Mix well together, aërate if required with carbonate of soda.

175   MILK LEMONADE.

Half a pound of pounded sugar ; one pint of milk ; one pint of water ; the juice of three lemons. Mix well together, and strain through a sieve.

176   LEMON WHEY.

One pint of boiling milk ; half a pint of lemon juice ; sugar to taste.   Mix well together and strain through a sieve.

177   LEMON SYLLABUBS.

One pint of cream ; one pint of water ; one pound of powdered sugar ; the thin peel of three lemons and the juice of one.   Whip up well with the white of one egg, and collect the froth off on a sieve.   When served, put the liquor in glasses and the froth on top.

178   IMPERIAL.

Half ounce of lemon peel ; half ounce cream of tartar ; four ounces of loaf sugar.   Bruise the lemon peel with the sugar, mix with the cream of tartar, then bottle.   When required for use, add one pint of boiling water.

179   KING'S CUP.

Peel of one lemon ; one and a half ounce lump sugar ; one pint of cold water ; a tea-spoonful of orange-flower water.   After ten hours infusion strain.

180   GINGER WINE.

Put twelve pounds of loaf sugar and six ounces of powdered ginger into six gallons of water, let it boil for an hour; then beat up the whites of half a dozen eggs with a whisk, and mix them well with the liquor.   When quite cold, put it into a barrel, with six lemons cut into slices and a cupful of yeast.   Let it work for three days, then put in the bung.   In a week's time you may bottle it, and it will be ready for immediate use.

181 RASPBERRY, STRAWBERRY, CURRANT, or ORANGE EFFERVESCING DRAFTS.

Take one quart of the juice of either of the above fruits, filter it, and boil it into a syrup with one pound of powdered loaf sugar ; to this add one ounce and a half of tartaric acid. When cold put it into a bottle and keep it well corked. When required for use, fill a half-pint tumbler three parts full of water, and add two table-spoonfuls of syrup. Then stir in briskly a small tea-spoonful of carbonate of soda, and a very delicious drink will be formed. The colour may be improved by adding a very small portion of cochineal to the syrup at the time of boiling.

LEO'S SPECIALITIES.

——:o:——

182 KOHINOOR.

On the edge of a large tumbler, break a new laid egg, upon which pour a liqueur glass of Benedictine, and a table-spoonful of raspberry syrup, shake up well with a little ice ; having done so, half fill with champagne ; balance with soda water, stirring at the same time with a spoon. Strain through a fine sieve, look heavenwards and drink ; "result," bliss.

183 MAGNOLIA (a la Simmons).

Beat up two new laid eggs ; add one liqueur glass of Curaçoa, and half a wine glass of old brandy ; one table-spoonful of sugar ; beat up well, then add a pint bottle of champagne, and mix by pouring from one glass to another until it attain a fleecy and soft appearance, and serve in a glass. This will be found a very nutritious drink, especially when the appetite is bad.

184 GIRARD FLIP.

So styled after the famous grotesque dancers of that name, being their favourite beverage when thoroughly exhausted after their terpsichorean eccentricities. In a tumbler place the yolk of an egg, to this add about a tea-spoonful of noyeau ; a dash of cayenne pepper ; a half glass of brandy ; a gill of ice. Fill up with new milk, shake well and strain.

185   CIDER NOGG.

Put in a large tumbler, a new laid egg, and one table-spoonful of powdered sugar. Stir up well with a spoon, and fill up with cider, and drink while effervescing.

186   CURAÇOA COCKTAIL.

Use small tumbler.

Half a wine glass of Curaçoa; half a wine glass of brandy; one tea-spoonful of Angostura bitters. Stir well with a spoon, add chipped ice and strain.

187   SQUARE MEAL.

The yolk of two eggs; pepper and salt to suit the palate; one glass of brown brandy; shake well in ice and strain. A good substitute for a Prairie Oyster.

188   PRAIRIE OYSTER.

This simple but very nutritious drink may be taken by any person of the most delicate digestion, and has become one of the most popular delicacies since its introduction by me at Messrs. Spiers and Pond's. Its mode of preparation is very simple. Into a wine glass put a new-laid egg; add half a tea-spoonful of vinegar, dropping it gently down on the inside of the glass; then drop on the yolk a little common salt, sufficient not to quite cover half the size of a threepenny-piece; pepper according to taste. The way to take this should be by placing the glass with the vinegar furthest from the mouth and swallow the contents. The vinegar being the last gives it more of an oyster-like flavour.

Note.—This can be taken with or without the white of the egg, according to taste.

189   OUR SWIZZLE.

It occurred to the Author of this little work, after a conversation with an Indian gentleman, to make a cocktail called in India a *Swizzle*. Take a small tumbler, half fill it with chipped ice; then add one and a half liqueur glasses of Boker's bitters; half a wine glass of brandy; and two or three drops of Noyeau to flavour and sweeten it. Now swizzle this concoction, with an Indian cane swizzle, to a froth; drink through a strainer. Tastes differ. An Indian likes a cocktail swizzled; a North American, within the last few years, will not take one unless it is stirred with a spoon; a South American will have it shaken; an Englishman, who has travelled in America, is more particular than any one of the others until you find out his taste, and is most difficult to please.

190   CRITERION REVIVER.

Use a Soda-water tumbler.

Glass and a half of Encore whiskey; small block of ice; dash of brandy bitters; bottle of Taunus water; and drink while effervescing.

191   BOSOM CARESSER.

Cobbler Glass.

One egg; half a sherry glass of strawberry syrup; one glass of brandy. Shake up well and strain.

192   ALABAZAM.

Use tumbler.

One tea-spoonful of Angostura bitters; two tea-spoonfuls of orange Curaçoa; one tea-spoonful of white sugar ; one tea-spoonful of lemon juice; half a wine glass of brandy. Shake up well with fine ice and strain in a claret glass.

193 CRITERION COFFEE PUNCH.

Use tumbler.

The yolk of one egg; small cup of black coffee (à la Criterion); liqueur glass of brandy; sweeten to taste. Shake up well with ice, and strain.

194 FLIP FLAP.

Fill up a sherry wine glass two-thirds full of Maraschino, yellow Chartreuse, Kummel in equal proportions, and one dash of Kirschenwasser. Having done this, add the white of an egg with a little sugar. Shake or swizzle well in a tumbler and serve in a thin glass.

195 HEAP OF COMFORT.

Use tumbler.

One new-laid egg; liqueur glass of Maraschino; liqueur glass of brandy; Cayenne pepper according to taste; gum syrup. Shake up well with ice and strain in a cocktail glass.

196 SHERRY BLUSH.

To a half glass of sherry add a tea-spoonful of Boker's bitters; the juice of half a lemon; a tea-spoonful of raspberry Noyeau and Vanilla, mix well up with shaved ice, and strain in an ornamented glass—a white glass is preferable, which, if dipped in coloured sugar, will make a pretty appearance. This is a very tasty little drink, and suitable after luncheon.

197 SODA NOGG.

Use large tumbler.

Break on the edge a new-laid egg; some pine-apple syrup; half a pint of shaved ice; fill up with soda, and imbibe through straws. A small quantity of brandy is a great improvement, according to taste.

198   LADIES' BLUSH.

Favourite Drink among the Fair Sex.

Use small tumbler.

To a wine glass of Old Tom gin add one tea-spoonful of Noyeau and five drops of Absinthe; sweeten to taste, about one tea-spoonful of white sugar.   Shake up well with shaven ice, strain, and pour into a coloured glass, the rim of which has already been damped with lemon juice and dipped in white sugar.

199   FLASH OF LIGHTNING.

Use tumbler.

A wine glass of brandy; half a tea-spoonful of gingerette; table-spoonful of raspberry syrup.   Shake up well with ice, and strain.

200   CRITERION FLIP.

One egg; glass of claret; two tea-spoonfuls of sugar; dash of Cayenne pepper. Shake well and strain.

201   "ENCORE" SADDLE ROCK.

This is a specie of Cobbler and is made the same way, substituting Encore Whiskey (the best for this purpose) instead of the wine of an ordinary cobbler.   With the addition of a little lemon juice you have a fine Saddle Rock.   It is a pleasant and cool drink for a summer's day imbibed through straws.

LARGE TUMBLER OR COBBLER GLASS.

202   LEO'S KNICKEBEIN.

Keep a mixture ready made to hand, thoroughly combined, of the following, in the proportions given:—One-third each of Curaçoa, Noyeau, and Maraschino. When mixing a drink, fill a straw-stem, port-wine glass two-thirds full of the above mixture, float the unbroken yolk of a new-laid egg on the surface of the liquor, then build up a kind of pyramid with the whisked white of the same egg on the surface of the latter, dash a few drops of Angostura bitters, and drink as directed.

DIRECTIONS FOR TAKING THE KNICKEBEIN.
Registered.

1. Pass the glass under the *Nostrils* and *Inhale* the *Flavour.*—Pause.

2. Hold the glass *perpendicularly,* close under your mouth, open it *wide,* and suck the froth by drawing a *Deep Breath.*—Pause again.

3. *Point* the lips and take *one-third* of the *liquid contents* remaining in the glass without *touching* the *yolk.*—Pause once more.

4. Straighten the body, throw the *head backward,* swallow the contents remaining in the glass *all at once,* at the same time *breaking the yolk* in your mouth.

———————

N.B.—All articles requisite in compounding mixed drinks, in the way of shakers or mixers, straws, &c., can be obtained of Messrs. DOWS CLARK & CO., Compton House, Frith Street, Soho.

THE AMERICAN BAR

AT THE

CRITERION

OPEN DAILY

From 12 to 12;   Sunday, 6 to 11,

UNDER THE MANAGEMENT OF

LEO ENGEL.

FRANK FLOWER,

DIAMOND MERCHANT,

3, PICCADILLY,

OPPOSITE THE "CRITERION."

LONDON "HALL MARKED"

18-CARAT GOLD CHAINS,

AT £3, 10s., PER OUNCE.

AND

THE CHARGE FOR MAKING ENTIRE CHAIN IS
20s.

ST. JAMES'S HALL,

PICCADILLY.

ALL THE YEAR ROUND,

THE

MOORE & BURGESS

MINSTRELS,

THE PREMIER COMPANY OF THE WORLD,

COMPRISING NO LESS THAN

FORTY ARTISTS

OF KNOWN EMINENCE.

EVERY NIGHT AT 8.

MONDAYS,
      WEDNESDAYS, } **3 and 8.**
           SATURDAYS,

Fourteenth Year in one unbroken Season.

T. FOXWELL,
Anglo-American Tailor,
56, JUDD STREET,
KING'S CROSS.

OPPOSITE THE GRAND ENTRANCE OF THE MIDLAND HOTEL.

THE ORIGINAL LEOPOLDS,

WILLIAM, JOHN,

AND

FREDERICK,

Gymnastic, Acrobatic and Grotesque

Artistes,

Of all the Principle Cirques and Theatres

in the world.

PERMANENT ADDRESS:

58, SPENCER STREET,

GOSWELL ROAD, LONDON, E.C.

THOSE PHENOMENAL FARCEURS,

THE GIRARDS,

The Premier and Original American Grotesque Dancers and Pantomimists.

Excerpta of Notices by the Australian, American, and English Press :—

"Let it at once be stated that their performances are far more extraordinary than they could possibly have appeared on paper, and perfectly unique."—*Melbourne Argus*, June 6th, 1874.

"As dancers of a novel gymnastic school, they have unquestionably no equals."—*New York Mercury*, April 12th, 1876.

"The Girards may now be pronounced without rivals ; one of them does the Long Table Slide, of which he was the original performer, having first introduced it to the public in the 'Black Crook' in Niblo's Garden, some few years ago."—*New York Clipper*, May 27th, 1876.

"To use a comprehensive old word, they are Posture Masters ; and never has more masterly posturing been seen in combination with neater pantomime of the grotesque kind, or with such continuance of surprising agility."—*Daily Telegraph*, August 28th, 1876.

"A more striking, original, and perplexing performance has never been seen."—*Sunday Times*, September 3rd, 1876.

"The Girards, a trio of dancers and pantomimic actors, who, for humour and agility, are not to be surpassed by any representatives of a similar class of entertainment who have appeared before a London audience."—*Daily News*, August 30th, 1876.

"The Girards, whose versatile ability, as exemplified in sundry very extraordinary and startling feats, is likely to add another to the list of 'Sensations' of late years introduced in the world of amusement. Their qualifications are of the most varied character."—*The Era*, September 3rd, 1876.

"To return to the piece, despite its pretentious title, of course the trifle is only a vehicle for the introduction of the Girards with their clever entertainment, about the marvellous excellence of which their cannot be two opinions. We would also refer to a certain Grotesque grace that now and again displays itself in the attitudes of this extraordinary family. Such a performance is one of the wonders of the age, and should attract all those who have not had an opportunity of witnessing it. Such of the public as have already seen the Girards will not need any words of ours to induce them to repeat the enjoyment upon an early occasion."—*The Era*, December 30th, 1877.

THE CRITERION,

PICCADILLY.

————:o:————

DEPARTMENTS.

BUFFET.—This elegant and popular lounge is open from 10 A.M. till 12.30 A.M., for the supply of hot and cold Luncheons, which can here be obtained at 1s. each and upwards ; and of Tea, Coffee, Ices, and all kinds of light Refreshments at the usual prices. Bass's Bitter Ale and Reid's Stout on draught. After 9 P.M. this department is reserved for Gentlemen only.

GRILL ROOM.—Open at all hours between 11 A.M. and midnight, and on Sundays from 6 P.M. till 10.30 P.M. Specially arranged for supplying both Ladies and Gentlemen with Luncheons, Dinners, and Suppers. Chops, Steaks, &c., from the Grill.

THE AMERICAN BAR, under the superintendence of a well-known Professor (originator of the famous Knickebein, &c.), has become one of the great attractions of the CRITERION. Choice of over 300 genuine American Drinks.

THE CIGAR DEPARTMENT is designed for an extensive wholesale and retail trade, and the stock, which is one of the largest in London, has been selected with unusual care. The attention of connoisseurs is confidently directed to its large assortment of every well-known brand of Havana and Manilla Cigars.

THE SMOKING ROOM is, *par excellence,* the most comfortable, most elegant, and best ventilated one in the Metropolis, and is now the principal West-end rendezvous of our Australian and American visitors.

THE RESTAURANT is arranged for the service of first-class Dinners, *a la Carte,* to both Ladies and Gentlemen. This room opens at 1 P.M. and closes at 9 P.M., and is open on Sundays from 6 P.M. *till 9 P.M.*

THE WEST ROOM is devoted to the DINNER PARISIEN (Winter season) from 5.30 till 8 P.M.; (Summer season) from 6 till 8.30 P.M., at 5s. per head. In order that the style and excellence of this Dinner may favourably compare with those of the best Restaurants in Paris, the services of an eminent Maître d'Hôtel have been secured, and under his superintendence the Dinners in this Room will be prepared and served entirely à la Française.

THE GRAND HALL is now occupied by the 3s. 6d. Table d'Hôte Dinner, served here daily from 5.30 till 8 P.M. (Winter season), and from 6 till 8.30 P.M. (Summer season). Separate tables for parties of two, three, or more. During the season the celebrated Cold Luncheon at 2s. 6d. per head is also served in this Room.

EAST ROOM.—Recherché Dinners, from 7s. 6d. upwards, served at separate Tables. This Room is especially adapted for Ladies and Gentlemen visiting the Opera or Theatre.

THE SOUTH ROOM is admirably adapted for Regimental, Masonic, and Presentation Dinners. This Room is also available for Masonic Lodges.

PRIVATE ROOMS of different sizes, wherein are daily served the most recherché Dinners in London.

These rooms are available for First-class Dinners to parties of not less than three.

For all information as to terms and arrangements, application should be made to the Manager.

THE THEATRE.—Attached to, and forming part of, the Establishment is the Criterion Theatre, open every evening. The entertainments are of a light and bright character, supported by the best available talent.

NOTE.—No Ladies are admitted to the Buffet after 9 P.M. With this single exception, the CRITERION in all the above Departments is opened to and designed for the patronage of Ladies as well as of Gentlemen.

————:o:————

SPIERS & POND.

48888696R00070

Made in the USA
Lexington, KY
16 January 2016